DAY HIKES IN
SUMMIT
COUNTY
COLORADO

by Robert Stone

Photographs by Robert Stone
Published by:
Day Hike Books, Inc.
114 South Hauser Box 865
Red Lodge, MT 59068
Layout & Design: Paula Doherty
Copyright 1997
Library of Congress Catalog Card Number: 96-96514

Distributed by:
ICS Books, Inc.
1370 E. 86th Place
Merrillville, IN 46410
1-800-541-7323
Fax 1-800-336-8334

TABLE OF CONTENTS

THE HIKES

About the Hikes

Colorado is known for the majestic Rocky Mountains that divide the North American continent. Running north and south, the Colorado Rocky Mountains contain 75 percent of all the land above 10,000 feet in the continental United States, including 1,000 peaks rising over 10,000 feet and 53 peaks rising over 14,000 feet. Forty percent of Colorado—over 23 million acres—is public land. 600,000 acres are designated to the state's 11 national parks, while national forests encompass 14 million acres. Colorado also has 37 state parks, 222 wildlife areas, and 25 designated wilderness areas. More than 100 rivers flow through the state, including the headwaters of four major rivers—the Arkansas, Colorado, Platt, and Rio Grande. There are 8,000 miles of streams, 2,000 lakes and reservoirs, thousands of miles of hiking trails, and hundreds of camp-grounds. The Rocky Mountains are home to bear, moose, elk, deer, antelope, big horn sheep, and mountain goats. Needless to say, outdoor recreation in Colorado is a way of life.

The Day Hikes guide to Summit County, Colorado, fo-cuses on scenic day hikes of various lengths. All of the hikes are in Summit County, located 80 miles west of Denver. Summit County is known for its ski resorts and the charming, historic towns of Breckenridge, Dillon, Frisco, Keystone, and Silverthorne.

The county in encircled by the Arapaho National Forest and straddles the Continental Divide. It is surrounded by the magnificent peaks of three mountain ranges—the Williams Fork, the Gore, and the Tenmile Ranges. The elevations of these mountains range from 8,000 to 14,000 feet. (The restored Victorian gold mining town of Breckenridge sits at 9,600 feet.) Although the weather is generally warm and sunny, the air can be cool at this altitude. Wind and afternoon thundershowers are common throughout the summer, so be sure to dress accordingly.

Summit County offers endless opportunities for outdoor recreation, such as fishing, bicycling, rafting, gold panning, horseback riding, golfing, or hiking. The county has an abundance of paved bike paths and miles of mountain trails, making the hiking in this area superb. There are more than 1,000 miles of streams (including the Blue and Snake Rivers), Dillon and Green Mountain Reservoirs, a multitude of high country alpine lakes, steep canyons with cascading waterfalls, and lush valleys covered in wildflowers. My goal is to share some of Summit County's hikes with you and others, providing visitors as well as locals easy access to the backcountry.

The two major access roads to these hikes are I-70, which runs east and west, and Highway 9, which heads north and south out of Silverthorne. These hikes are detailed on the United States Geological Survey topo maps that are listed with each hike and can be purchased at most area sporting goods stores.

All of these hikes require easy to moderate effort and are timed at a leisurely rate. If you wish to hike faster or go further, set your own pace accordingly. As I hike, I enjoy looking at clouds, rocks, wildflowers, streams, vistas, and any other subtle pleasures of nature. While this adds to the time, it also adds to the experience.

As for attire and equipment, tennis shoes, as opposed to hiking boots, are fine for any of these hikes. Layered clothing, a rain poncho, a hat, sunscreen, mosquito repellent, and drinking water are recommended. Pack a lunch for a picnic at scenic outlooks, streams, or wherever you find the best spot.

Enjoy your hike!

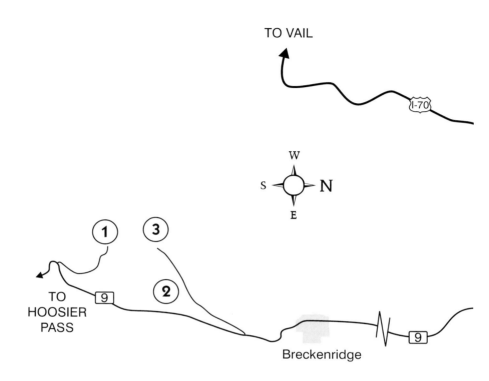

TO VAIL

I-70

W
S — N
E

① ③

TO
HOOSIER
PASS

9 ②

Breckenridge

9

MAP OF

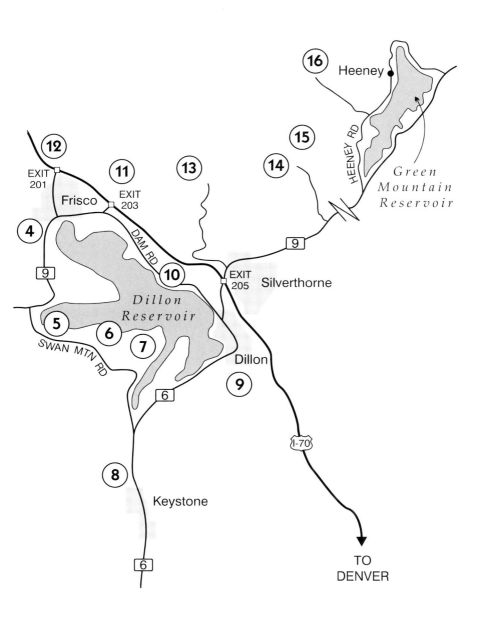

THE HIKES

Hike 1
McCullough Gulch

Hiking Distance: 2.8 miles round trip
Hiking Time: 2.5 hours
Elevation Gain: 1,000 feet
Topo: Trails Illustrated #109 Breckenridge/Tennessee Pass
U.S.G.S. Breckenridge

Summary of hike: This hike offers majestic cascading water and waterfalls (cover photo). The fields are often covered with an abundance of wildflowers. Above the waterfall is a beautiful glacial lake.

Driving directions: From the south end of Breckenridge, drive 7.6 miles south on Highway 9. Turn right on Blue Lakes Drive #850, and continue 100 yards ahead to McCullough Gulch Road. Turn right and drive 2.2 miles to the end of the road, staying left at the Y-junction, and park.

Hiking directions: From the trailhead, walk up the old jeep trail and around the gate. About 15 minutes up the trail is a road junction. Take the left fork. (The right fork leads to private property.) Continue on the footpath through a pine forest and several stream crossings to the roaring, tumbling cascades. It will be hard to resist exploring around the rocks and the various levels of the falls and cascades (photo on page 18). Afterwards, return to the trail, and follow it to the lake above the falls. Throughout this hike, various other trails connect with the main trail. They all lead to the falls and return back to the trailhead.

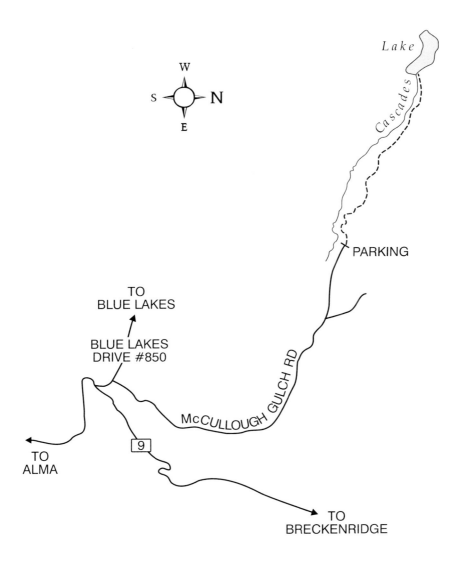

W

S —⊕— N

E

Lake

Cascades

PARKING

TO
BLUE LAKES

BLUE LAKES
DRIVE #850

McCULLOUGH GULCH RD

9

TO
ALMA

TO
BRECKENRIDGE

McCULLOUGH GULCH

Hike 2
Spruce Creek Trail

Hiking distance: 3.7 miles round trip
Hiking time: 2 hours
Elevation gain: 650 feet
Topo: Trails Illustrated #109 Breckenridge/Tennessee Pass
U.S.G.S. Breckenridge

Summary of hike: The Spruce Creek Trail parallels Spruce Creek upstream. The trail leads to a beaver pond in a meadow surrounded by stunning mountain peaks (photo on page 23). The forested trail includes two footbridges that cross Spruce Creek.

Driving directions: From the south end of Breckenridge, drive 2.3 miles south on Highway 9. Turn right on Spruce Creek Road, just past the lake on the left. Continue up Spruce Creek Road 1.2 miles to the trailhead parking area. Along the way, the road winds through the Crown Subdivision.

Hiking directions: From the parking area, take the footpath on the left side of the road at the Spruce Creek Trail sign. The trail follows Spruce Creek through the forest. Although there are smaller side trails, stay on the main trail. The trail crosses Spruce Creek via a footbridge at 0.7 miles. Continue upstream to the Wheeler Trail junction. The last half mile gains more elevation. Twenty steps past the junction is a large beaver pond in a beautiful meadow with the Tenmile Mountain Range as a backdrop. Take the Wheeler Trail about 100 feet to the right to another bridge over Spruce Creek. This is our turn-around spot. Return along the same trail.

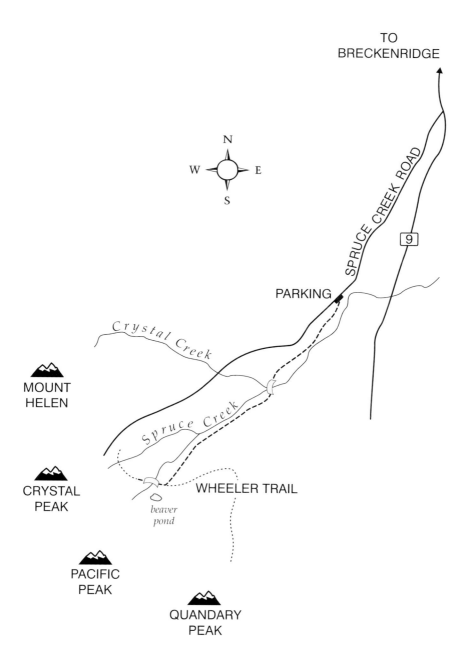

TO
BRECKENRIDGE

N
W · E
S

SPRUCE CREEK ROAD

9

PARKING

Crystal Creek

MOUNT
HELEN

Spruce Creek

CRYSTAL
PEAK

WHEELER TRAIL

*beaver
pond*

PACIFIC
PEAK

QUANDARY
PEAK

SPRUCE CREEK TRAIL

Hike 3
Mohawk Lakes and Continental Falls

Hiking Distance: 3 miles round trip
Hiking Time: 3 hours (includes side trips to various levels
          of the waterfall and the old log cabins)
Elevation Gain: 1,200 feet
Topo: Trails Illustrated #109 Breckenridge/Tennessee Pass
          U.S.G.S. Breckenridge

Summary of hike: This hike is a steady climb past beautiful
lakes, endless braids of cascading water, a spectacular waterfall, old log mining houses, and views of the valley and
mountains. The Mohawk Lakes sit at an elevation of 12,000
feet.

Driving directions: From the south end of Breckenridge,
drive 2.3 miles south on Highway 9. Turn right on Spruce Creek
Road, just past the lake on the left. Continue on Spruce Creek
Road as it winds through the Crown Subdivision. Continue 2.8
miles to the trailhead parking area. At 2.6 miles, the road goes
noticeably downhill. The parking area is around the bend at the
bottom of this hill.

Hiking directions: From the parking area, hike up the road
about five minutes to the trailhead, just past the green Forest
Service storage sheds. The trail begins to the right at the
posted sign. One hundred yards further, take the left trail. This
trail follows Spruce Creek (photo on page 19). Along the way,
many short side trails lead to various views of Continental Falls.
Upon reaching Lower Mohawk Lake, the trail continues to the
left towards Mohawk Lake. To return, follow the same path.

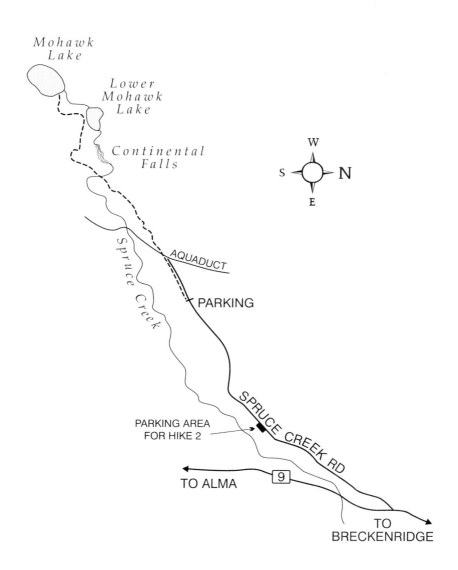

Mohawk Lake

Lower Mohawk Lake

Continental Falls

W
S ✦ N
E

Spruce Creek

AQUADUCT

PARKING

PARKING AREA FOR HIKE 2

SPRUCE CREEK RD

← TO ALMA

9

TO BRECKENRIDGE →

MOHAWK LAKES

Hike 4
Peaks Trail
along Miners Creek

Hiking distance: 5 miles round trip
Hiking time: 2.5 hours
Elevation gain: 400 feet
Topo: Trails Illustrated #109 Breckenridge/Tennessee Pass
U.S.G.S. Breckenridge

Summary of hike: Located close to the town of Frisco, this portion of the Peaks Trail follows the cascading Miners Creek along the Tenmile Range. The hike is easy and passes an abundance of beaver ponds.

Although the Peaks Trail is ten miles in length and connects Frisco with Breckenridge, this hike only follows the first portion of the trail as it parallels Miners Creek.

Driving directions: From I-70, take the Breckenridge Exit #203 east for 1.7 miles towards Breckenridge on Highway 9. Turn right on Road 1004 and drive 0.1 mile to a road fork. Take the right fork 0.2 miles to the trailhead parking area at the end of the road.

Hiking directions: From the parking area, walk up the paved bike path 0.1 mile to the bike crossing. Cross the bike path to the trailhead sign and take the Miners Creek Road, a gravel road to the left. The trail quickly enters an aspen and pine forest. Continue past the Forest Service gate. At 0.5 miles, Miners Creek will be flowing alongside the road. A well-defined but unmarked path will be on the left. The footpath, Peaks Trail, follows Miners Creek for the next two miles to the Miners Creek Trail Junction. Although the trail continues, this junction is a good place to begin retracing your steps.

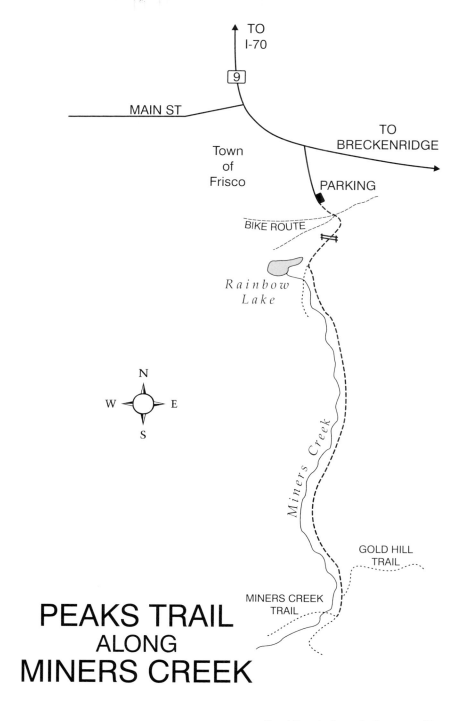

TO
I-70

9

MAIN ST

TO
BRECKENRIDGE

Town
of
Frisco

PARKING

BIKE ROUTE

*Rainbow
Lake*

N
W E
S

Miners Creek

GOLD HILL
TRAIL

MINERS CREEK
TRAIL

PEAKS TRAIL
ALONG
MINERS CREEK

Hike 5
Dillon Reservoir
Blue River Arm Fisherman Trail

Hiking Distance: 2.5 miles round trip
Hiking Time: 1 hour
Elevation Gain: Level hiking
Topo: Trails Illustrated #108 Vail/Frisco/Dillon
U.S.G.S. Frisco

Summary of hike: This fisherman trail begins as a beautiful river walk through lodgepole pine forests. It continues along the lake to sandy beaches.

Driving directions: From I-70, take the Breckenridge Exit #203 east, passing over the interstate. Drive 4.2 miles towards Breckenridge on Highway 9. Turn left at Swan Mountain Road, the first turn past Dillon Reservoir. As you cross over the stream, the parking area is on the right.

Hiking directions: From the parking area, cross Swan Mountain Road towards the lake. Stay to the right (east) of Blue River. The trail is easy to spot and stays close to the river, then weaves along the shoreline. The first sandy beach is located where Blue River flows into the arm of Dillon Reservoir. There are additional sand beaches along the way.

As you near Sapphire Point, the trail begins to climb along the cliff edge and becomes harder to follow. Although the trail continues, this is our turnaround spot. Return along the same route.

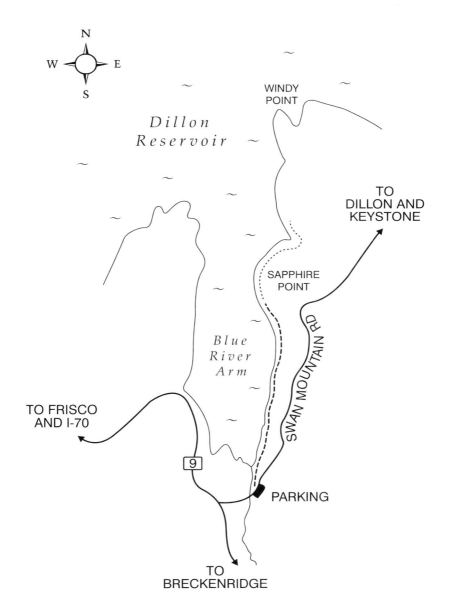

N
W E
S

~ ~ ~

WINDY
POINT

*Dillon
Reservoir* ~

~

~

~

TO
DILLON AND
KEYSTONE

~

SAPPHIRE
POINT

~

*Blue
River
Arm*

SWAN MOUNTAIN RD

TO FRISCO
AND I-70

~

9

PARKING

TO
BRECKENRIDGE

DILLON RESERVOIR
BLUE RIVER ARM FISHERMAN TRAIL

Cascading water at McCullough Gulch - Hike 1

Clouds over Lower Boulder Lake - Hike 15

The trail alongside Lower Cataract Lake – Hike 16

Spruce Creek enroute to the Mohawk Lakes – Hike 3

Hike 6
Sapphire Point Loop

Hiking distance: 0.8 mile loop
Hiking time: 20 minutes
Elevation gain: Level hiking
Topo: Trails Illustrated #108 Vail/Frisco/Dillon
         U.S.G.S. Frisco

Summary of hike: This 0.8 mile loop is a gentle meander through the forest at an elevation of 9,600 feet. The trail offers panoramic views of Dillon Lake, the towns of Frisco, Dillon, and Silverthorne, plus the Gore, Tenmile, and Williams Fork Mountain Ranges. The views are breathtaking in every direction. Picnic tables and benches are located throughout the loop.

Driving directions: From I-70, there are two routes to the trail:
    1) Take the Breckenridge Exit #203 east, passing over the interstate. Drive 4.2 miles towards Breckenridge on Highway 9. Turn left at Swan Mountain Road. Continue 1.8 miles to the Sapphire Point parking lot on the left.
    2) Take the Silverthorne Exit #205 east, passing under the interstate. Drive 4.5 miles towards Keystone to Swan Mountain Road. Turn right and continue 3 miles to the Sapphire Point parking lot on the right.

Hiking directions: From the parking lot, take the trail on the left past the restroom. A short distance ahead is an overlook with sweeping views of the Tenmile Mountain Range and the Blue River Arm of the reservoir. The trail then curves to the right, offering the Gore Mountains to the west, the town of Frisco, and the many islands in the reservoir. The trail loops back to picnic benches and views to the north, which include the town of Dillon beneath the shadows of the Williams Fork Mountains. The trail soon loops back to the parking area.

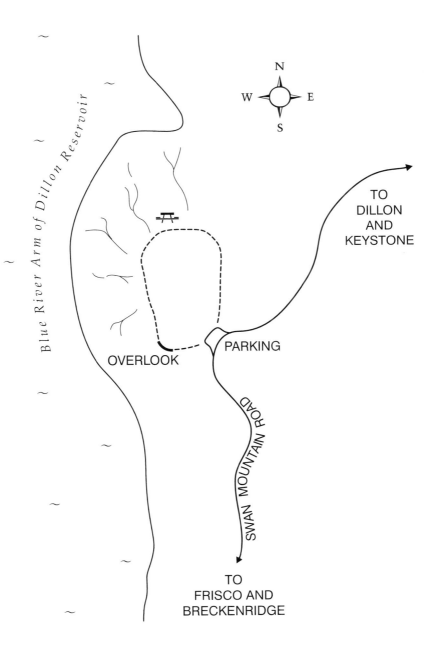

Blue River Arm of Dillon Reservoir

N
W E
S

TO
DILLON
AND
KEYSTONE

PARKING

OVERLOOK

SWAN MOUNTAIN ROAD

TO
FRISCO AND
BRECKENRIDGE

SAPPHIRE POINT LOOP

Views from the Rock Creek Trail - Hike 14

Lily Pad Lake - Hike 13

Learning to fish at Old Dillon Reservoir – Hike 10

Chester swimming in the beaver pond – Hike 2

Hike 7
Windy Point Lakeshore Trail

Hiking distance: 1.5 mile loop
Hiking time: 1 hour
Elevation gain: Level hiking
Topo: Trails Illustrated #108 Vail/Frisco/Dillon
        U.S.G.S. Frisco

Summary of hike: The Windy Point Trail is an easy and scenic loop along the Dillon Reservoir shoreline. The trail winds through a lodgepole pine forest enroute to the shore.

Driving directions: From I-70, there are two routes to the trail:
   1) Take the Breckenridge Exit #203 east, passing over the interstate. Drive 4.2 miles towards Breckenridge on Highway 9. Turn left at Swan Mountain Road, the first turn past the Dillon Reservoir. Continue 2.8 miles to the Swan Mountain Recreation Area/Prospector Campground on the left—turn left.
   2) Take the Silverthorne Exit #205 east, passing under the interstate. Drive 4.5 miles to Swan Lake Road on the right—turn right. Continue 2 miles to the Swan Mountain Recreational Area/Prospector Campground on the right—turn right.
      Drive 0.5 miles to the campground entrance. Turn left and park in the trailhead parking area on the right.

Hiking directions: The trailhead is at the far end of the parking area. The trail leads through the campground and lodgepole pine forest to a clearing with a view of the lake on the left. Take the trail to the left that leads to the water's edge. Just before reaching the water, the trail leads to the right, looping around the perimeter of Windy Point to a cove. Picnic facilities and restrooms are located here. Walk past the facilities. The trail picks up again, leading back to the parking area and completing the loop.

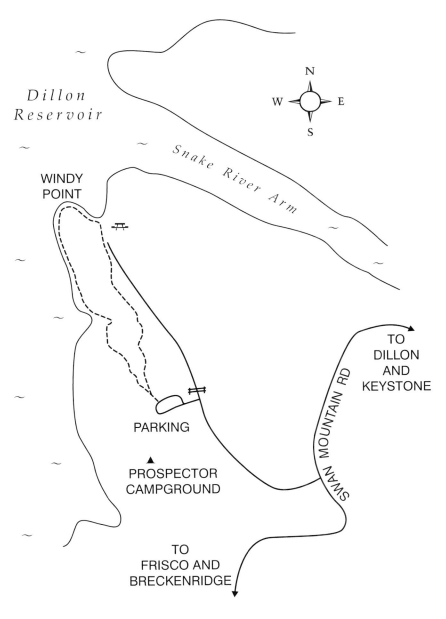

Dillon
Reservoir

Snake River Arm

N
W   E
S

WINDY
POINT

TO
DILLON
AND
KEYSTONE

SWAN MOUNTAIN RD

PARKING

▲
PROSPECTOR
CAMPGROUND

TO
FRISCO AND
BRECKENRIDGE

WINDY POINT
LAKESHORE TRAIL

Hike 8
Snake River to Keystone Lake

Hiking Distance: 3.2 miles round trip
Hiking Time: 2 hours
Elevation Gain: Level hiking
Topo: Trails Illustrated #104
          Idaho Springs/Georgetown/Loveland Pass
          U.S.G.S. Keystone

Summary of hike: This is a beautiful walking and bicycling path that winds along the north side of the Snake River. The hike ends in the town of Keystone at Keystone Lake.

Driving directions: From Keystone, drive west (toward Dillon) on Keystone Road/Highway 6. The parking turnout is 1.1 miles from the last stoplight in town. It is on the south side of the highway where the Snake River crosses under the road.

Hiking directions: From the parking area, walk past the buck fence and follow the footpath to the left towards Keystone. The trail parallels the Snake River to a charming lake with a picturesque boathouse. Kayaks, canoes, and paddle boats may be rented. To return, follow the same path back to your car.

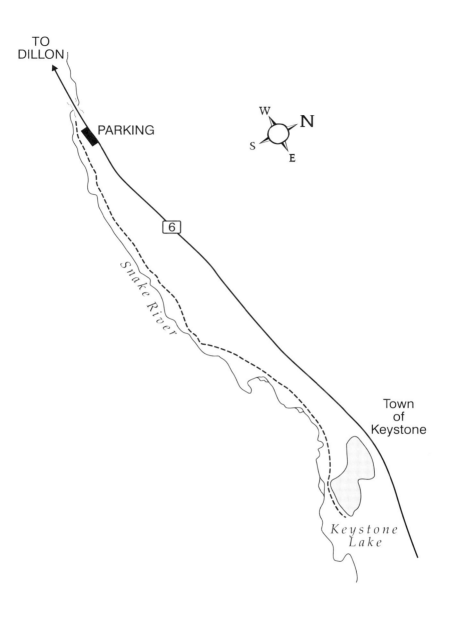

TO
DILLON

PARKING

W N
S E

6

Snake River

Town
of
Keystone

Keystone
Lake

SNAKE RIVER
TO KEYSTONE LAKE

Hike 9
Tenderfoot Trail

Hiking Distance: 2 miles round trip
Hiking Time: 1 hour
Elevation Gain: 500 feet
Topo: Trails Illustrated #108 Vail/Frisco/Dillon
            U.S.G.S. Dillon

Summary of hike: This mountain hike winds through an aspen and lodgepole forest. There are magnificent views of Dillon, the Gore and Tenmile Mountain Ranges, and the reservoir (photo on back cover).

Driving directions: From I-70, take the Silverthorne Exit #205. Turn south and drive under the interstate toward Dillon on Highway 6. Drive 1.2 miles to Lake Dillon Drive. Turn left; then take an immediate right. Continue 0.7 miles to the trailhead parking area, just beyond the water tower. The trailhead is well marked.

Hiking directions: From the parking area, hike past the water treatment building to the jeep road/trail. After five minutes of hiking, the Tenderfoot Trail branches off to the left. A trail sign will direct you. Continue on the trail as you gradually climb to the excellent views of Dillon, Frisco, Silverthorne, Dillon Lake, the Tenmile and Gore Ranges, and the Continental Divide. A bench is well placed on this elevated perch to oversee the view and allow rest. A second bench is placed on the hill with views towards Keystone and Loveland Pass. This viewing area is our turnaround spot. For those who wish to keep walking, the trail continues to the top, but it does become steep. To return, retrace your steps to the trailhead.

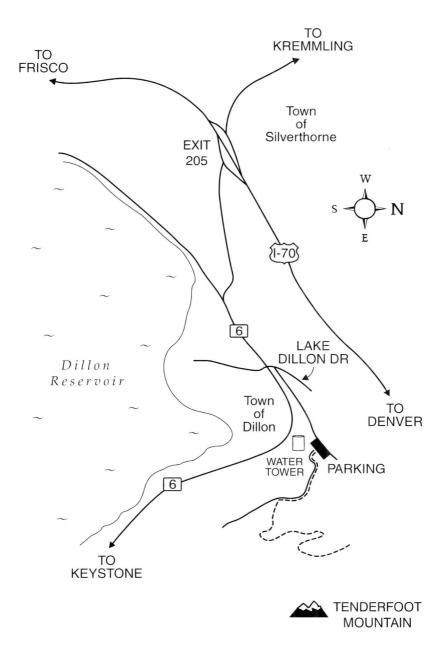

TENDERFOOT TRAIL

Hike 10
Old Dillon Reservoir Trail

Hiking Distance: 1.5 miles round trip
Hiking Time: 1 hour
Elevation Gain: 140 feet
Topo: Trails Illustrated #108 Vail/Frisco/Dillon
         U.S.G.S. Frisco

Summary of hike: This easy hike circles a three-acre reservoir (photo on page 23) with fantastic views of Dillon Reservoir. The hike also has views of the Continental Divide and the surrounding Swan, Tenmile, Tenderfoot, Gore, and Williams Fork Mountains.

Driving directions: From I-70, take the Breckenridge Exit #203 east, passing over the interstate. Turn left at the first light onto Dam Road. Drive 1.6 miles on Dam Road to the reservoir parking lot on the left (west) side of the road. Turn left and park.

From Frisco, drive towards I-70. Turn right at Dam Road, just before the interstate. Drive 1.6 miles on Dam Road to the reservoir parking lot on the left side of the road.

From Dillon, go southwest towards Frisco on Dam Road. Drive two miles to the reservoir parking lot on the right (west) side of the road.

Hiking directions: From the parking lot, start at the trailhead sign. This well-marked trail curves to the right (northeast) through a ponderosa and lodgepole pine forest. The trail loops around Old Dillon Reservoir. Upon completing the loop, retrace your steps back to the trailhead.

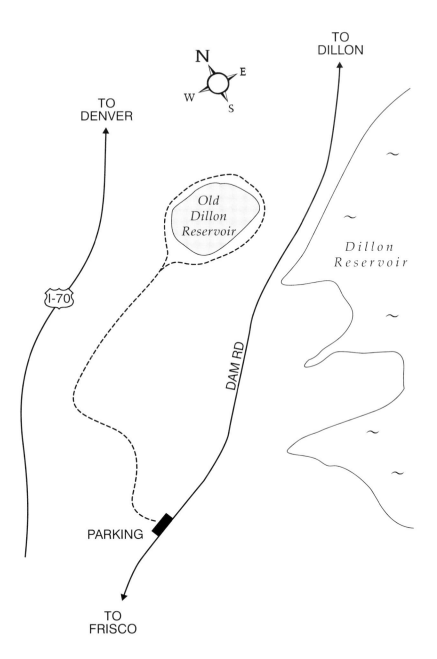

TO
DILLON

N
E
W
S

TO
DENVER

Old
Dillon
Reservoir

Dillon
Reservoir

I-70

DAM RD

PARKING

TO
FRISCO

OLD DILLON RESERVOIR

Hike 11
Meadow Creek Trail
to Lily Pad Lake

Hiking distance: 1.6 miles round trip to bridge
2.5 miles round trip to Lily Pad Lake
Hiking time: 1 hour to 1.5 hours
Elevation gain: 340 feet to bridge / 500 feet to lake
Topo: Trails Illustrated #108 Vail/Frisco/Dillon
U.S.G.S. Frisco

Summary of hike: The Meadow Creek Trail follows a clear, tumbling mountain creek through an aspen and lodgepole pine forest. The trail climbs gradually but steadily to a bridge that crosses Meadow Creek. The trail continues to the south and east shores of Lily Pad Lake.

Driving directions: From I-70, take the Breckenridge Exit #203 west, away from Frisco, for about 100 feet. Turn left onto the gravel road. Drive 0.5 miles to the trailhead parking area at the end of the road.

Hiking directions: From the parking area, the posted trailhead is easy to see. The trail climbs into an aspen forest to a trail junction. Stay left and cross a log footbridge. At 0.6 miles is a trail junction, located just after the remains of an old mining cabin on the left. Although the Meadow Creek Trail continues straight ahead, take the Lily Pad Lake Trail to the right. Continue 0.2 miles to the bridge over Meadow Creek. This bridge is the turnaround spot for the shorter hike.

For those who wish to continue to Lily Pad Lake, the trail gently climbs 0.4 miles to the south shore of the lake. The trail winds along the east shore to a pond. Although the trail continues to a trailhead at the Wildernest Subdivision (Hike 13), this is our turnaround point. Return on the same path.

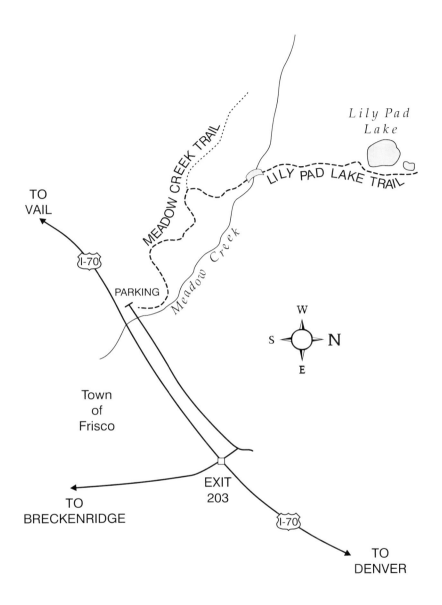

MEADOW CREEK TRAIL
TO
LILY PAD LAKE

Hike 12
North Tenmile Creek Trail

Hiking distance: 4 miles round trip to Wilderness Boundary
7 miles round trip to Gore Range Trail Jct.
Hiking time: 2 hours to 3 hours
Elevation gain: 600 feet to 800 feet
Topo: Trails Illustrated #108 Vail/Frisco/Dillon
U.S.G.S. Frisco and Vail Pass

Summary of hike: The North Tenmile Creek Trail parallels the creek up the glacially carved canyon, sandwiched between Chief Mountain on the right and Wichita Mountain on the left. Although the first two miles follows an old jeep trail, this is a lush wilderness experience. The trail passes through a dense forest, open meadows covered in wildflowers, beaver ponds, and stream crossings. The creek is within view at all times.

Driving directions: From I-70, take the Frisco Exit #201. Turn west, away from Frisco, and park in the trailhead parking area 100 feet ahead.

Hiking directions: From the parking area, walk up the road past the metal fence and water tank. Along the first mile, the trail parallels the turbulent North Tenmile Creek as it tumbles down the canyon. Most of the elevation gain takes place here. Although there are various trails forking off the main trail, they all connect. Staying close to the creek will keep you on the mail trail.
 The trail levels off after one mile. There are open meadows and many beaver ponds. At two miles is the Eagles Nest National Forest Wilderness Boundary. The trail becomes a footpath here. This is the turnaround spot for the four-mile round trip hike.
 The next turnaround spot is 1.5 miles ahead at the Gore Range Trail junction. This portion of the trail crosses an abundance of small streams that join the North Tenmile Creek. Return along the same trail after reaching the junction.

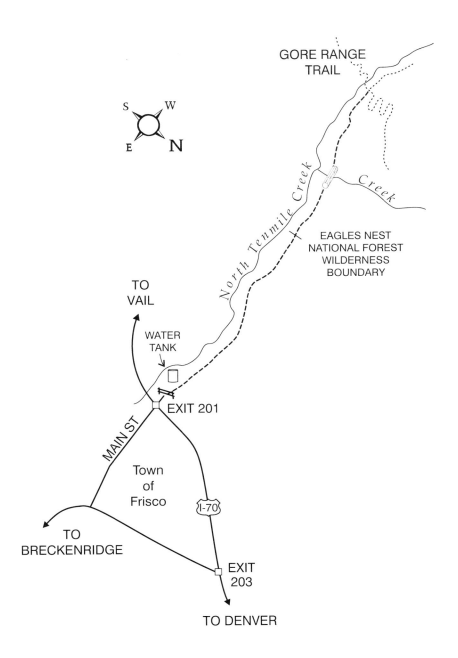

NORTH TENMILE CREEK TRAIL

Hike 13
Lily Pad Lake

Hiking Distance: 3 miles round trip
Hiking Time: 1.5 hours
Elevation Gain: 200 feet
Topo: Trails Illustrated #108 Vail/Frisco/Dillon
        U.S.G.S. Frisco

Summary of hike: This is a beautiful hike to two lakes. The first lake is covered in yellow-flowered lily pads (photo on page 22). The second, and much larger lake, is deep blue in color with mountains as a backdrop. The trail passes by streams, a beaver pond, and through aspen and pine forests at the base of Buffalo Mountain.

Driving directions: From I-70, take the Silverthorne Exit #205. Drive 0.2 miles north on Highway 9 to Wildernest Road and turn left. Drive 3.5 miles to the end of this road, which turns into Ryan Gulch Road. At the end, the road begins to loop. Park at the top of this loop on the left.

Hiking directions: Hike up the old road that is chained off to vehicles. Stay to the right at the top of the hill when the road becomes a footpath. The trail winds around the left side of a beaver pond and across a log bridge over the stream. Other small trails will appear throughout this hike. The main trail will lead to both lakes. Although the trail continues past Lily Pad Lake to the Meadow Creek Trail (Hike 11), the lake is our turnaround spot. Return on the same trail.

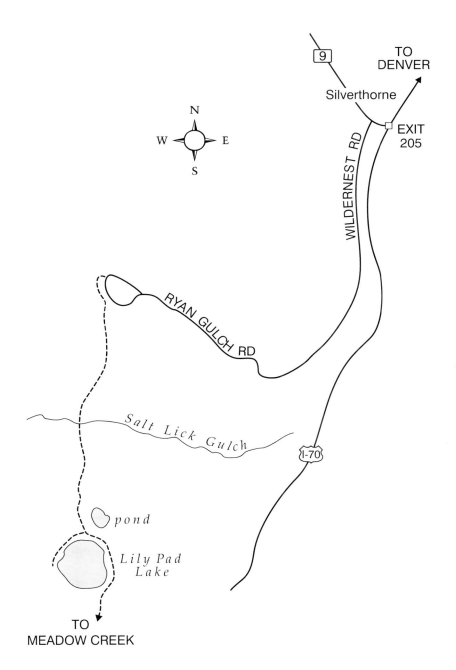

LILY PAD LAKE

Hike 14
Rock Creek Trail
to Boss Mine

Hiking distance: 3 miles round trip
Hiking time: 2 hours
Elevation gain: 600 feet
Topo: Trails Illustrated #108 Vail/Frisco/Dillon
U.S.G.S. Willow Lakes

Summary of hike: The Rock Creek Trail parallels Rock Creek enroute to the remnants of the Boss Mine, a silver mine dating back to the 1880s. Along this forested route to the mine are beaver ponds and a bird nesting sanctuary. A photo of the view along the trail is on page 22.

Driving directions: From I-70, take the Silverthorne Exit #205. Drive 7.3 miles north on Highway 9. Turn left on Rock Creek Road, across the highway from the Blue River National Forest Campground. Drive up Rock Creek Road 1.3 miles and turn left towards the Rock Creek trailhead. Continue 1.5 miles to the end of the road. Park at the trailhead.

Hiking directions: From the parking lot, walk up the main road past a metal gate to a well-marked "Gore Range Trail" junction. Continue straight ahead on the main trail. A series of beaver ponds will be on your left. At 0.75 miles, the trail enters the Alfred M. Bailey Bird Nesting Area, teeming with the sound of birds. The old jeep road narrows and begins to climb gently. At 1.3 miles is a small stream crossing by a hillside covered with tailings from the mine. The trail becomes steeper and begins a series of switchbacks. At the end of the trail are remnants of the mine and house. Beyond this point, the trail is covered in loose rock and is not recommended. To return, retrace your steps.

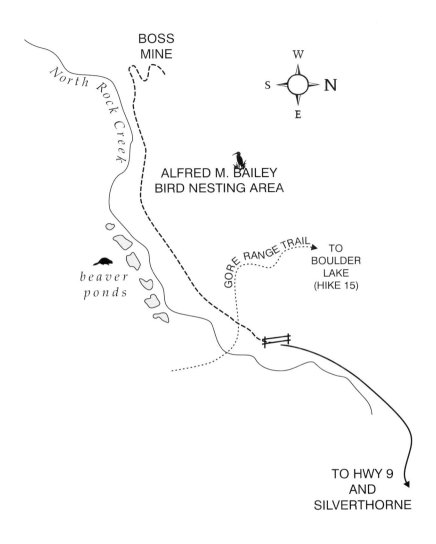

BOSS
MINE

W
S ⊕ N
E

ALFRED M. BAILEY
BIRD NESTING AREA

North Rock Creek

GORE RANGE TRAIL

TO
BOULDER
LAKE
(HIKE 15)

*beaver
ponds*

TO HWY 9
AND
SILVERTHORNE

ROCK CREEK TRAIL
TO
BOSS MINE

Hike 15
Lower Boulder Lake

Hiking Distance: 5 miles round trip
Hiking Time: 3 hours
Elevation Gain: 500 feet (up and down several times)
Topo: Trails Illustrated #108 Vail/Frisco/Dillon
U.S.G.S. Willow Lakes

Summary of hike: This trail passes through a forest canopy of lodgepole pines to the Boulder Creek drainage and a magnificent 10,000-foot high lake (photo on page 18). From the lake are sweeping views of snow-peaked mountains.

Driving directions: From I-70, take the Silverthorne Exit #205. Drive 7.3 miles north on Highway 9. Turn left on Rock Creek Road, across the highway from the Blue River National Forest Campground. Drive up Rock Creek Road 1.3 miles and turn left towards Rock Creek trailhead. Continue 1.5 miles to the end of the road. Park at the trailhead.

Hiking directions: From the parking lot, walk up the main road past a metal gate to a well-marked "Gore Range Trail" junction. Take the right (north) trail about two miles to the Boulder Creek Trail junction. There is an abundance of ups and downs on this trail. At the Boulder Creek Trail, take the left trail, and head upstream for 0.3 miles to Lower Boulder Lake. To return, retrace the many ups and downs back to the trailhead.

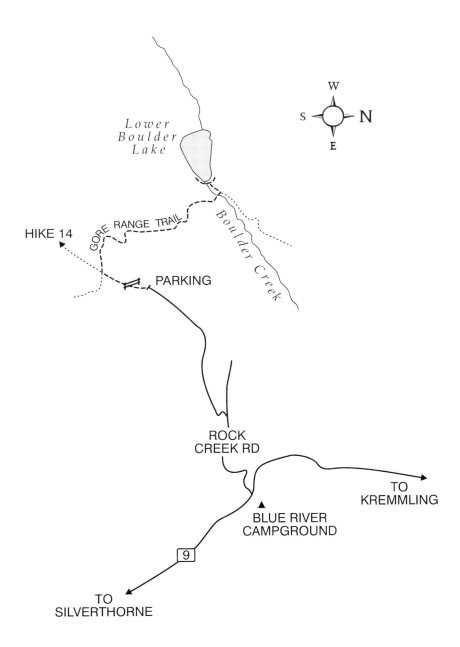

Lower Boulder Lake

GORE RANGE TRAIL

Boulder Creek

HIKE 14

PARKING

W
S — N
E

ROCK CREEK RD

TO KREMMLING

▲
BLUE RIVER CAMPGROUND

9

TO SILVERTHORNE

LOWER BOULDER LAKE

Hike 16
Lower Cataract Lake Loop

Hiking Distance: 2 miles round trip
Hiking Time: 1 hour
Elevation Gain: 150 feet
Topo: Trails Illustrated #107
Green Mountain Reservoir/Ute Pass
U.S.G.S. Mount Powell

Summary of hike: This trail circles Lower Cataract Lake through evergreen and aspen forests. It includes panoramic views down canyon and of the surrounding mountains. Cataract Creek Falls can be seen across the lake, dropping 300 feet down the cliffs.

Driving directions: From I-70, take the Silverthorne Exit #205, and drive 16.5 miles north on Highway 9. Turn left onto Heeney Road #30. A sign on the highway will direct you. Continue on Heeney Road 5.4 miles to County Road 1725 and turn left. Drive 2.6 miles to the Lower Cataract Lake parking area. This parking area is on the right, just past the campground.

Hiking directions: Walk to the end of the parking area and past the gate to the trailhead. Take the trail to the far left, hiking clockwise around the lake (photo on page 19). This is the beginning of the loop. At the far end of the lake is a bridge crossing over Cataract Creek. The trail continues around the other side of the lake back to the trailhead.

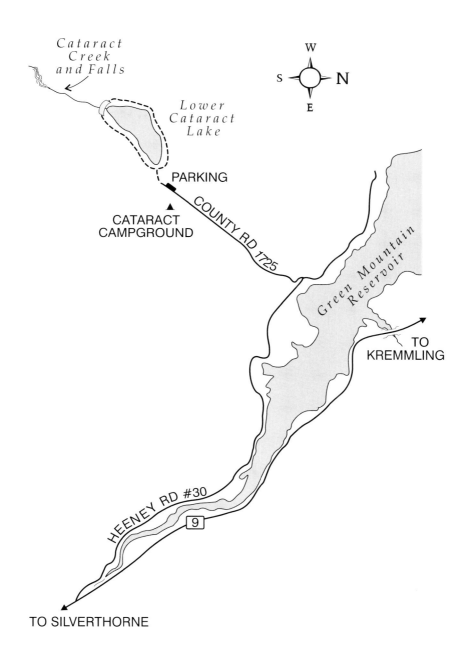

Cataract Creek and Falls

Lower Cataract Lake

W
S ✦ N
E

PARKING

COUNTY RD 1725

▲
CATARACT
CAMPGROUND

Green Mountain Reservoir

TO
KREMMLING

HEENEY RD #30

9

TO SILVERTHORNE

LOWER CATARACT LAKE

NOTES

Information Sources

Town of:
  Breckenridge   (303) 453-2251
  Dillon   (303) 468-2403
  Frisco   (303) 668-5276
  Silverthorne   (303) 468-2637

Summit County
  Chamber of Commerce
P.O. Box 214
Frisco, CO 80443
(303) 668-5800

Summit County
  Chamber of Commerce
Dillon, CO 80435
(303) 468-2403

Breckenridge Resort Chamber
P.O. Box 1909
Breckenridge, CO 80424
(303) 453-6018

Colorado Parks & Recreation
1313 Sherman St.
Denver, CO 80203
(303) 866-3437

Colorado Tourism Board
1625 Broadway Suite 1700
Denver, CO 80202
(800) 433-2656
(303) 592-5510

Summit County
  Central Reservations
(800) 365-6365
(303) 468-6222

Other Day Hike Guidebooks

___ Day Hikes on Oahu $6.95
___ Day Hikes on Maui 8.95
___ Day Hikes on Kauai 8.95
___ Day Trips on St. Martin 9.95
___ Day Hikes in Denver 6.95
___ Day Hikes in Boulder, Colorado 8.95
___ Day Hikes in Steamboat Springs, Colorado 8.95
___ Day Hikes in Summit County, Colorado 8.95
___ Day Hikes in Aspen, Colorado 7.95
___ Day Hikes in Yosemite National Park
      25 Favorite Hikes 8.95
___ Day Hikes in Yellowstone National Park
      25 Favorite Hikes 7.95
___ Day Hikes in the Grand Tetons and Jackson Hole, WY 7.95
___ Day Hikes in Los Angeles
      Malibu to Hollywood 8.95
___ Day Hikes in the Beartooth Mountains
      Red Lodge, Montana to Yellowstone National Park 8.95

These books may be purchased at your local bookstore or they will
be glad to order them. For a full list of titles available directly from
ICS Books, call toll-free 1-800-541-7323. Visa or Mastercard accepted.

- -

Please include $2.00 per order to cover postage and handling.
Please send the books marked above. I enclose $_____

Name _____

Address _____

City _____ State _____ Zip _____

Credit Card # _____ Exp. _____

Signature _____

1-800-541-7323

Distributed by:
ICS Books, Inc.
1370 E. 86th Place, Merrillville, In. 46410
1-800-541-7323 · Fax 1-800-336-8334

TOM EGENES

About the Author

The lure of the beautiful Rocky Mountains drew Robert to Red Lodge, Montana, in 1979. Hiking, exploring, and living in the Rockies has fulfilled a lifelong dream.

Robert Stone has traveled and photographed extensively throughout Asia, Europe, the Caribbean, Hawaii, and the Continental United States.